KNOWING GOD

Wiley Bumgarner

Publisher: Ralph Roberts

Editor: Pat Roberts

Cover Design: ©2001 Ralph Roberts
Interior Design & Electronic Page Assembly: **WorldComm®**

10 9 8 7 6 5 4 3 2

Printed by QUESTprint

ISBN 1-57090-125-2

Mountain Church—a division of Creativity, Inc.—is a full–service publisher located at 65 Macedonia Road, Alexander NC 28701. Phone (828) 252–9515, Fax (704) 255–8719. For orders only: 1-800-472-0438. Visa and MasterCard accepted.

Mountain Church is distributed to the trade by Midpoint Trade Books, Inc., 27 West 20th Street, New York NY 10011, (212) 727-0190, (212) 727-0195 fax.

This book is also available on the internet in the **Publishers CyberMall.** Set your browser to http://www.abooks.com and enjoy the many fine values available there.

CONTENTS

About The Author

Wiley C. Bumgarner is a native of Haywood County, North Carolina. He was born in Waynesville, North Carolina on March 22, 1919.

Wiley is the son of the late Julius Pinkney Bumgarner and Julia Lanning Bumgarner. Wiley had seven brothers, all older than he and two sisters. One sister, who is still living, is younger than he is. His brothers and older sister are all deceased.

Wiley grew up on a small farm during the Great Depression. He worked several years as a construction worker before serving in the U.S. Navy throughout World War II.

After the War, Wiley attended Mars Hill College, Furman University, Southern Baptist Theological Seminary, and Arizona State University.

Wiley has pastored Baptist churches, has taught history and English, and has served as a realtor.

Wiley lives with his wife, Hazel, to whom he has been married since February 17, 1946. They reside in Asheville, North Carolina.

Wiley and Hazel have one son, Barry, and three grandchildren.

Foreword

I have written these articles during periods of meditation and study. I read and interpret Scriptures and then write down the interpretation from memory in my own words. I sometimes recall the Scripture or some other wise saying exactly as it has been written, but I do it from memory. I almost never copy what someone has written.

I read the Bible in different versions, but I am not concerned with the literal words. I always concern myself with what I believe to be the meaning of what is written. When I make an interpretation, I draw from all my knowledge and experience. I believe that truth and God are always in agreement. I care not where the truth comes from. It is my desire to know truth and apply truth to life. I also believe that all falsehood is against God. I use the term Satan to refer to falsehood or deception. I believe that truth enhances life and that falsehood takes away from life.

I believe that we are to make learners of people. Whatever we do with our lives we will accomplish more if we seek knowledge, understanding and wisdom. I hope that by reading and thinking about what I have written, you, the reader, will live a more abundant and more enjoyable life. I hope you come to know the truth that sets one free. May you become free from ignorance, superstition, falsehood, and ill will. May these writings help you to turn from Satan unto God.

Work, Morality and Self-righteousness

I learned when a teenager that living for Christ is dying to self.

To be a follower of Christ is to think of what we are doing and how to do it right. It is not to be self-centered.

A good worker thinks of what he is producing not of what he is getting for himself.

A good worker thinks of the outcome not of the income.

A self-centered person is never happy, content, or fulfilled.

A self-centered person is never right with God, others or himself.

A self-centered person is always trying to reform others.

A self-centered person is always an actor or pretender.

A self-centered person is always sensitive.

A self-centered person is concerned about victory or defeat.

God is not someone or something to be acted upon.

God is reality. Reality is what is regardless of circumstances.

God is eternally present.

God is the only constant.

God is the eternal, ever present law, which governs or controls the universe.

It is concepts of God that change, not God.

God is what we attribute to him at any given time from our view. But the reality is what is.

God works through life and action.

If we serve God and fulfill his purposes, we try to discover him and obey him.

It is the folly of fools to try to change or manipulate God.

It is also the folly of fools to try to glorify oneself or seek God's praises.

We cannot flatter God. Being or acting pious is vain glory.

It is the nature of children to seek attention. It is always a sign of immaturity.

It is also immature to try to change others, except by example. If you want others to do something, you teach them to do it by rewarding their efforts.

Things and people that are true to their purpose make life better. Falsehood or disloyalty makes life worse.

We make a better world when we help others.

We make the world worse when we take by greed or coercion what belongs to others.

Forget about yourself and start thinking about how you can be helpful to humanity.

Forget how the machinery looks, or what people think of how it looks, and start thinking of the product.

Creating a product is beyond looking at the means of production. The right machinery is the machinery that can be used in the production of the product. What good does it do for something to be good if it is good for nothing?

Self-righteousness is not worth anything. The world existed before I came. It will exist when I am gone. It is what I contribute while I am here that counts.

So called prayer is usually wasted words spoken for vain glory. We try to change reality when we should try to know, understand, and inspire.

Jesus did not die so that we could have a home in Heaven. Jesus died so we could have a heavenly home. We have a heavenly home when we love one another and forget ourselves. We gain life when we lose it. We lose life when we try to hoard it. The happy person gives out. The unhappy person tries to take in.

Jesus tells us to die daily to self. Quit trying to look important to get applause and start living for the benefit of humanity.

Learn to obey the laws of God and to make life better for others. It is love not greed that praises God.

Prayer is facing reality not seeking escape. Do the best with what you have, where you are, and the future will fall in place. "Study to show yourself approved unto God a workman that needeth not to be ashamed rightly dividing the word of truth."

When we study each situation and try to find the reality, we are acting wisely. We cannot avoid truth, but we do have to learn how to apply it. Our mission is to apply our time, talents, and influence so as to help our fellow beings live abundant lives. By helping others our own needs are supplied. If we constantly think of ourselves we deprive everybody. The self-centered person will die. Die to self and find salvation.

Prayerful Learning (2 Tim 2:15)

The only way to do a good job is to learn how the job is to be done before we start doing it. We must be humble enough to suffer through the process of learning. We must suffer in the flesh during the learning process. Life is not all pleasure. Discipline precedes pleasure or reward. Children enjoy pretense or make believe. Adults are more sincere.

Humble people learn and make progress. When things are done right progress is made. Proud people exalt themselves and, after appearing to be doing right at first, are later found to have no foundation. The humble learners are exalted.

The proud pretenders or play actors are put down. An airbag or balloon is easily burst. When we are assigned a task, we should seek to do it right. The discipline of learning precedes doing the task. The humble discipline themselves.

The disciplined learner builds on firm foundations. The proud actor or pretender is more interested in applause. Proud pretenders choose balloons as symbols. They like to be seen, but their egos are what show. They major on externals.

The Kingdom of Heaven is built on a firm foundation. Only the proud fools build on the sand. Daniel did not become next to the King because he was foolish. He was the wisest man in Babylon at the time. King Solomon was a wise man.

If one desires to do a great job, he tries to learn the best way to do it. "Fools rush in where Angels fear to tread." Those who speak without knowledge are worse than fools. They cause others to perish along with themselves. Jesus is said to have said, "Those who lead others astray would be better off drowned."

All permanent work is well planned. Great oaks take a while to grow. Oak is good building material. Mushrooms grow fast, we sometimes eat them. It takes time to develop character. It takes time and self-discipline to acquire wisdom. We get wisdom from those above or beyond us. The ultimate source is God or the best.

Prayer is sincerity. If we are sincere, we humble ourselves and learn truth. The proud like to look good rather to be good. Instead of going into a private closet and seeking truth, they like to be seen in public places with a pious look. The proud do not fear god. They fear the public. The humble learn to do right. The proud learn to appear to do right. The humble build character. The proud seek applause.

Sincere or prayerful learning is the key to permanent success. The desire to learn is the beginning of wisdom. The desire to learn is the fear or respect for God. The desire to learn is humility. Humility leads to greater and better experiences. The process of learning leads to a more abundant life. The mission of the church is to make learners or disciples. The followers of Jesus were called disciples or learners. The Kingdom of God is built by knowledge, understanding, and wisdom. To accept Christ is to become a learner so as to attain knowledge, understanding, and wisdom.

We cannot proclaim truth until we know truth. When we show that we know truth, people will judge that we know Jesus.

Jesus has been called the Son of God and the Prince of Peace. When we become followers of Jesus, we will be peacemakers, and will be called children of God. Warmongers are not peace-makers. They do not employ the means of peace. They employ weapons of war. Let us follow Jesus and do some prayerful learning.

The Way of the Lord (1)

Jesus of Nazareth, whom we Christians accept as our Lord, is "The way, the truth, and the Life." The Jesus way is not just the best way, but for us it is the only way. Jesus personifies All that is good, right, true, and lasting.

To accept Jesus as Lord is to become a citizen of the Kingdom of God. Citizens of God's Kingdom accept as a way of life all that is good, right, true and helpful. We reject in principle all that is evil, wrong, false, or harmful.

Jesus reveals God as the Lord of Life. God is all we need or could hope for. God is an eternal principle of all that is love, good, right, true, and abiding. God is eternally present. He has no beginning and no ending. Eternity as a concept is the now of our time. The eternal God is the God of the present. Eternal life is the life of the present. We cannot live in the past, nor can we live in the future except in our dreams and visions. The reality is now.

God as this eternal principle of life is with us from the time we are born until we die. Birth puts us in touch with God. Death separates us from God. The Scriptures indicate that God gives us life when we are born and takes it away when we die.

Spiritual life begins when we accept Jesus as Lord and ends when we reject him as Lord. Jesus will not abide with us when we habitually dwell in sin. However, if and when we repent of sin, he will come again. Sin separates us from the eternal principle of the good, right, true, and abiding which we call God. God separates from sin. God saves or redeems. Sin destroys. The difference between good and evil, right and wrong, true and false, enduring and decaying is that what is Godly is redemptive and what is Satanic is destructive.

The way of Jesus as he reveals God is the way of peace. Those who make peace are the children or offspring of God. Those who engender strife are against God and his revealer, Christ Jesus. To believe in Jesus as Lord is to seek peace and harmony which comes about when we all love one another.

We who believe in the Jesus way believe in one God, and one humanity. We believe that God as an eternal ever present principle of all that is good, right, true, and enduring applies or is available to all people everywhere at all times. We are all one humanity or one species. Those among us who contribute most to enrich life are the greatest among us. "Life does not consist in the abundance of possessions." Life is somewhat reciprocal. We tend to get out of life what we put into it. If you want a better life; then, try to make life richer for others. Your blessings come through your vision of others. Your problems usually arise from the person reflected from the mirror.

When life is unsatisfactory, it needs to be renewed not just added onto. Sometimes a new garment or some good wine may help. We should not try to add patches to worn out garments. Nor should we refuse fresh ideas or methods. The fear of the Lord is the desire to learn, which is the beginning of wisdom. The wise live richer lives.

The way of the Lord is the way to a better, more righteous, truer, and more enduring life.

If we believe in Jesus, we seek to overcome ignorance, superstition, falsehood, and all other hindrances to a more abundant life. We seek to become peacemakers who will be called the offspring of God. If we are true peacemakers or true children of God, we will help others and ourselves to become healthier, wealthier, and wiser. And, thus, to live more abundant lives. May we sincerely or prayerfully seek, the way of the Lord.

The Glory

The Glory of the Lord is the inspiration of people of good will. The "Glory of the Lord" is the manifestation of truth or reality. When we glorify God, we make known the truth or reality. The manifestation or glory of God is making known what will work and what won't work. It is always wise to live and work in harmony with truth or reality. A person who is sane or is in his right mind does not try to do the impossible.

To seek a miracle instead of facing reality shows the lack of judgement or reality. It is evil or insane to pursue the impossible. To trust in God is to believe in his faithfulness. If God worked contrary to his laws, he would be unfaithful and knowing him or making him known would be of no value. To try to do the impossible is idolatry. It is as stupid as expecting help from a dumb idol. Idolatry leads to destruction. It is as foolish as deliberately doing what one knows is deadly. If there is anything clear to a sane person of good will, it is the fact that truth prevails. We cannot change reality. If we try to destroy reality, we make known that we are to that extent insane.

We speak of God as that person, power, or influence that is truth or reality. We believe that truth or reality is what is to be revealed in the making of wise decisions. We speak of what is against truth or deceptive as being ungodly, Satanic, or devilish. We speak of the word of God as being truth and love or good will.

Devil or Satan personifies all that is deceitful or of ill will. Deceit is always ill will and thus against God or what is good.

To tempt a person is to try to lead the person astray. It is always evil to tempt someone. It is especially evil to tempt an innocent, immature, or naïve person.

God cannot be led astray. To try to lead God astray is to have a false concept of God. It simply means that to try to tempt God is evidence that one does not know God. To do things contrary to reality means that there is no glory of God to that person. The one who attempts the impossible does not know God.

All knowledge, understanding, and wisdom helps one to know and accept reality or truth. The fear of the Lord has been interpreted to be the desire to learn or to know truth or reality. Humility has been defined as, "the beginning of wisdom."

Ignorance, superstition, falsehood, ill will and pride are enemies of God. The above are all overcome by the glory or knowledge, or manifestation of truth or reality, which we call God. To know God through actual experience is to live. When we come to know God is when we come to know and accept reality. The more truth or reality we know, the better we know God.

Jesus of Nazareth identified himself as the way, the truth, and the life. He identified his mission as the revelation of God so that all of us may come to have a more abundant life. Jesus teaches us that to know the truth or reality is to be set free.

Think of all the human effort and resources that are available to help us gain knowledge, understanding, and wisdom. Truth or reality is being revealed to all who are willing to learn. All sane people are learners. The great commandment of

Jesus is, "Go into all the world and make learners or disciples. Teach them to know God and to obey his laws." What Jesus means is that we are to reveal God or reality. It is experiencing truth that enriches life.

Next time you think of avoiding truth and seeking a miracle, stop and think. It is written, "Thou shalt not tempt the Lord, thy God."

"Be not deceived." If you would be free from evil, learn and accept truth. No sane person wants to be a slave to evil.

One God of All

I believe in one perfect God whose laws are unchangeable and pertain to the total population of the whole earth. If every human being lived in harmony with the laws of God; we would live in harmony with one another and would have peace and prosperity.

Obedience to the laws of God would lead to a more abundant life for each person. To obey the laws of God, we must have the mind of Christ. This means becoming completely unselfish. It means having vision and love that enables us to do unto others as we would have others do unto us. The one who has the mind of Christ is a redemptive person. The redemptive person is unselfish. That person has been redeemed from sin or selfishness. To that person life is no longer under external control. The redeemed person is controlled by the universal laws of God, which rule from within. The redeemed person's God is not a local baal, but the God of all people. The redeemed person is not a permanent child with a "me, my, and mine" philosophy. The redeemed person is freed from bonds of ignorance, superstition, falsehood, legalism, and literalism. The redeemed person who has the "Mind of Christ" has vision of a world without borders or walls. To the redeemed; we are limited only by our lack of faith in God.

I believe in Christ - a messiah who gave himself for the benefit of others. Jesus Christ whom the Christians follow is our Lord and Redeemer. Jesus teaches us that life is reciprocal. It is what we give freely that comes back to us. What we try to hold on to is taken away. We do reap what we sow. If we remain childishly selfish, we live limited lives. If we remain as we are born physically, we will have limited lives full of trouble.

Jesus put it right to Nicodemus when he said, "You must be born again." We must mature to the place where we are unselfish. We must reject all local baals and worship the one true God.

The redeemed person seeks the redemption of others. To be redeemed is to be set free. One is free when one knows the truth. The truth is the only real authority. Jesus personifies truth. He is the revelation of the one universal God who is eternal. Eternity is now. It has no beginning and no end. God's laws are eternally present and unchangeable. God's laws apply to all people, everywhere, at all times.

To be redeemed is not to be bound, but to be freed. Those who break the laws are imprisoned. Those who obey the laws of God are free. When we sin by disobeying the laws of God, we are enslaved. When we repent, we are set free.

"Believe in the Lord Jesus Christ and be set free." Worship some idol and you will be enslaved. The enslaved person lives within walls. The free person lives without walls. America is a great country. We have no walled cities. We worship no local gods or baals. We are free to travel as long as we obey our laws. As long as we are one nation under one God, we will remain a free people. When we start forcing religious beliefs on others, we become enslaved. We are enslaved by walls of separation. If we believe in Jesus, the Christ, we are set free. In Christ there are no walls of separation. Jesus says, "I am the way, the truth, and the life." "Come unto me and be saved." "Whosoever will may come." "Know the truth and the truth will set you free." "Be not deceived, God is not mocked; you reap what you sow." "Do unto others as you would have them do unto you." "Deny yourself." "Follow me."

The Promised Land

Those who believe in God, as he is revealed by Jesus the Christ, look forward to living in peace.

When we live in peace we are no longer at war with one another. We do not think of people as either friends or enemies. When we live in peace we think of people as fellow human beings, all having equal rights. When we are at peace with ourselves, we can live in peace with others.

When Joshua crossed the Jordan, he met a man with a drawn sword who was neither friend nor enemy. He was commander of the army of the Lord. People who serve the Lord are peace loving people. They are of character like that of Jesus the Christ.

The commander of the army of the Lord said to Joshua, "Take off your warrior boots and sit a spell."

It is no coincidence that Jesus is a descendant of Rahab, the young woman who negotiated with the spies of Joshua. If we are to save our lives and the lives of our families in time of war, we have to know how to negotiate. Jesus, being a descendant of Rahab, was a negotiator rather than a warrior. Jesus teaches us to negotiate with enemies rather than get ourselves killed.

When we are living in peace, we do not look for someone to fight but for someone whom we can serve. Real living is not having a contest to see who can win and who will be defeated. Life in Christ is not the "thrill of victory or the agony of defeat." Life in Christ is a joyous fellowship of human beings who love and serve one another.

When we accept Jesus Christ as Lord and Saviour, we seek unity. We, as followers of Jesus, love our neighbors as we love ourselves. We are not at enmity—two armed camps fighting one another.

Followers of Jesus believe in one God and one humanity. We are all for one and one for all. If God is with us, we are all winners. If we are against God, we are all losers. Victory in Christ is not found in destruction, but in negotiation.

Jesus Christ is not a descendant of Cain or Able. He is a descendant of Seth. When we fight and kill we do not serve nor have true fellowship.

The world honors its heroes. The church honors its martyrs. Jesus the Christ was crucified. He was more than a conqueror.

Jesus is not known for the many whom he has killed. He is known for being the Saviour. Jesus teaches us to negotiate rather than fight. "Second Mile" living is a lot better than killing the enemy.

When followers of Jesus meet a stranger, they do not ask, "Are you a friend or enemy?" We assume with Jesus that if they do not take action against us; they are for us. Owning a sword does not make one a friend or enemy.

If we follow Jesus, we will have few special friends or enemies. We will have many whom we treat as equals.

When we live in peace, we can have prosperity and hope. We don't need walls around our cities. Peace loving people can go and come as they wish as long as they respect the rights of others.

Followers of Jesus are peacemakers. They are called children of God. They are not known for their military conquests nor for their athletic defeats. They are known for their service to mankind.

If you want to brag about your ancestors, remember Jesus. He had the honor of having, as an ancestor, a woman who has been called a prostitute or harlot. She knew how to negotiate with the enemy to save the lives of her family. Jesus learned that it is better to die for what is right than to kill to save oneself. But when possible we should negotiate.

When we reach the Promised Land, let us decide whom we will serve. Our goal is not conquest but fellowship. Let us be as brothers who dwell in unity.

Sin (I)

God is the term we use to describe all that is real and in harmony with health, peace, and prosperity. Sin is everything that is against God.

To so live as to have health, peace, and prosperity is to live in obedience to all the laws of God.

Heaven is the term we use to portray the blissful experience that results from perfect obedience to all of the laws of God.

To live in harmony or obedience to all the laws of God is the goal of all mature thinking, sane, understanding people of good will.

The people who face reality seek to know, understand, and obey the laws of God. The laws of God are the ever present or eternal principles that cannot be changed. These principles are equal to or synonymous with God. They are what Jesus of Nazareth seeks to reveal. They are the eternal, unchanging, present principles that the followers of Jesus, whom we call The Universal Church, seeks to reveal. They are the principles that are at the base of all truth.

To live by faith is to believe in and seek to obey these principles which we call the laws of God. We are faithful to the extent that we consistently obey these laws.

To obey the laws of God is to learn to know and face truth or reality. We can only be faithful in doing something to the extent that we believe it is the right thing to do. When wedo not believe, we doubt. When we doubt, we need more knowledge, understanding, or wisdom. Faith is derived from knowledge, understanding, and wisdom.

The fear of God, or respect for God, or truth, which we call reality, is the desire to learn.

Ignorance, superstition, falsehood, ill will and everything else that are against truth are Satanic or sinful.

The goal of Jesus and his followers is to inspire, teach, and lead people to face truth with good will. The ultimate goal is perfect obedience to the laws or principles, which control the universe. To live in obedience to all the principles which control the universe is to experience Heaven or live with God.

To live by faith is to be faithful or consistent in doing what one believes is right. It is based on ones goals, knowledge, and understanding. Living by faith is living with a good conscience.

To have a good conscience one must be without a sense of guilt. To be without a sense of guilt one seeks to correct what is wrong. To correct what is wrong is to repent of sin. Sin is whatever is against truth or reality or good will.

As long as we know something is lacking, we feel guilty. If we feel guilty or uneasy, we cannot be completely at peace. When we feel guilty, we need to seriously seek to know what is wrong and, if possible or practical, correct it. If one has unconfessed sins, he or she cannot have a good or clear conscience.

Thus we can understand that God is what is right or real, and sin is what is wrong or unreal.

Living by faith is making one's own decisions and doing what one believes in with good will toward all people.

When one believes that God is reality or perfection and seeks to live in harmony with God, that person lives by faith.

Jesus commands us to become learners and teachers and to seek to live in harmony or obedient to the laws of God.

"Whether you eat or drink or whatever you do, do it to glorify God." We glorify God when we face truth and live in obedience to the ever present, unchanging laws of God. When we live by faith we glorify God and overcome sin.

God is the Spirit of truth or reality. Satan represents deception or untruth. God is light. Satan is darkness. God is positive. Satan is negative. When we do right and seek truth we glorify God and defeat Satan. Light overcomes darkness. Jesus is the light. He is the truth that sets us free.

If we know Jesus and believe in him we overcome sin. If we do not know Jesus and repent not of sin we will face destruction. Sin destroys. Jesus saves!

I Am

The prevailing truth is the I am which we call God. God is the term we use for reality or truth.

Those who seek truth and/or reality are those who seek God. Anyone who seeks to deceive is Satanic. God is all that is true, righteous, good, Holy, complete, helpful, loving, and enduring. Satan represents all that is deceptive or untrue–all that is against God.

Jesus Christ is "The way, the truth, and the life." Jesus reveals truth or reality. If one believes in Jesus Christ, he or she seeks to know and obey the laws of God. To know and obey the laws of God is to follow Jesus or live as he lives. To live in accordance with the laws of God is to have faith in Jesus Christ. It is written, "The righteous shall live by faith."

To live by faith is to obey the laws of God. To obey the laws of God is to face reality and do what is beneficial to all concerned. It means to have good will toward all people without deception of any kind.

Those who live by faith prove all things and hold to what is good. To live by faith in God as he is is to resist the temptation to deceive or allow oneself to be deceived.

To the follower of Jesus, the final authority is truth or God. The authority is reality. God is. Reality is what is. God is eternally, "I am." Reality is eternally or always present. With reality or God there is no beginning and no end.

God is the eternal or always present principle that controls all reality.

The laws of God have always existed and will always exist. We are always being judged by God's laws. We are responsible for our own lives and the lives of those in our care.

All sane, sober, and mature people of good will seek to know and obey the laws of God.

It is the insane, inebriated, immature, or those with ill will who seek to deceive.

The fear of God is the fear of doing wrong or the respect for doing right. The fear of God is the beginning of wisdom. The purpose of all education is to learn what is right and wrong. Before we can have wisdom, we must acquire knowledge and understanding. Thus the beginning of wisdom is the desire to learn. Those who never learn are ignorant, superstitious, and foolish.

To follow Jesus is to be a learner and to apply what one learns with good will. A follower of Jesus becomes a learner and a teacher. The follower of Jesus acquires the character of Jesus and becomes an example for others to follow. The follower of Jesus seeks ultimate or final truth, and never willfully takes part in deception.

Jesus teaches us to face truth and show good will. His final command is to make learners who will face reality and seek truth with good will.

Jesus is the Son of God. He faces reality from birth to death. Jesus personifies truth and good will. Jesus is the standard by which we are judged.

Ultimately each of us will be judged by what we say, do, and produce. Every one will be judged impartially. Reality or truth is what is. Eternity is what is always present. God is the always present reality. His laws are always present. Eternal life is always present life. The only eternal life is the present life. No one can live in the past or in the future. The only life is the life now. Try living some other time.

Face reality! Do it now or never. "Today is the day of salvation." These days are always the last days. They are also the first days. "Today is the first day of the rest of my life." The past and future meet in the present. "Now is the accepted time." Make the best of your life now!

When we face reality, we die to sin. Sin is deception.

The world is filled with deception. We continue to learn truth as long as we live. We never know all there is to know. To continue to learn is to remain humble. Since the room for improvement is the greatest room, humility is the greatest virtue. Pride is being conceited or deceived. Therefore, pride is the worst of sins.

Humility is the road to knowledge, understanding, and wisdom. Humility helps one take the first step upward. The humble enjoy being helpful or showing good will.

We are ultimately judged by our being helpful or not being helpful to others. The world existed before we came. It will be here when we are gone. Let us be good stewards while we are here. Let us serve the God, "I am." "Here, I am; send me."

The Name of Jesus

The name of Jesus is as the name of God. Jesus teaches us that God or reality is unlimited. God or reality cannot be limited to any people or place. With reality there is no space or time. What is is. Nothing can be excluded from reality. It is only our faith that is limited.

Human beings have always been able to go beyond common expectations when led by people of intelligence and ability. Leaders are out front. They do not follow the crowd or popular thinking or lack of thinking.

The law of Moses sets limits on what people are to do. Moses knows that he is dealing with slave minded people. They are people who serve rather than people who lead. Instead of being free people who think and share their thoughts, they are dominated by the thinking of Moses.

No people who depend on the thinking of others can advance beyond the thinking of their leaders. Slaves, like prisoners, are walled in by the thinking of the strong men among them whom they regard as Lords or Lord.

Free people are unlimited. The greatest room in the world is the room for improvement. Think of all the progress that has been made by free people. Think of the speed of progress in our day. We are emphasizing communication and progress.

Think of how little progress was made during the Dark Ages when the Catholic Church dominated society. Even yet, churches put more emphasis on ritual and ceremony than on progress. The Fundamentalists of the world prevent progress. They say they have the Bible as their guide. They worship or follow the great Bible interpreters instead of thinking for themselves. They follow Moses more than Jesus.

Moses presents God as the author of the laws, which Moses gives to the people. In the laws of Moses people are limited to the thinking of Moses. All the laws or regulations come from the top down. The people are not allowed to think and act freely. They are asked to obey Moses as the man of God.

To the Fundamentalist, obedience to the leaders in authority is the essence of righteousness. No new ideas or practices are allowed.

To Jesus, each individual is allowed to think. We are intelligent beings capable of thinking and proving what is best. Jesus called this living by faith. When we live by faith we think seriously about life, prove all things, and hold to what is good.

"Without faith it is impossible to face truth." Puppets or mechanical things know nothing of truth. Slaves and non-thinkers follow others rather than seek to discover truth. Jesus tells us to know the truth. To know truth we have to prove what is true.

Jesus advocates truth. To Jesus, truth is the only authority. When we know the truth we are no longer slaves to ignorance, superstition, and falsehood. We who know the truth reject falsehood. Jesus represents truth. Satan is the name for deception or falsehood. When we do something in the Name of Jesus, we do it in the name of truth. To accept Jesus is to accept truth. To know Jesus is to know truth. To have the Spirit of God is to have the Spirit of truth.

To serve God or face reality we must be free to think and free to do what is good, right, and true.

God's word is truth. God is reality. God is on the side of truth. The enemy of God is the lack of truth. The concept of Satan as the enemy of God is very simple. Anyone or anything that hinders truth is against god.

When we are right with god, we are in touch with reality. A demoniac is one who is out of his mind or out of touch with reality. Our serious thoughts or prayers lead us to truth and good will. God is reality or truth. Our serious thoughts or prayers help us to find the will of God.

The will of God is whatever is beneficial to humanity.

All the real improvements in the world are beneficial to humanity. God is real. God is good. God is just. God is eternal. God is present. God is love. Our need is more faith in God. We gain faith by proving what is good and then working for the benefit of humanity.

Worshipping God is not living by what some group of people has written as truth, but worshipping God is having a Spirit of truth and love. It is attributing worth to what is true or real. It is refusing to be deceived or to deceive others. We need more faith in truth and more knowledge of truth.

"Know the truth and the truth will set you free." "In the name of Jesus" is "In the name of truth." Truth is the glory of God. Let us glorify God. Always seek truth or "pray without ceasing." In Jesus' Name or Character.

The Bread of Life

Jesus presents himself as the Bread of Life. He shares his knowledge, and understanding, and wisdom. It is the mental strength that makes us different from the other animals. Mental strength is Spiritual strength. It is through the mind that we experience God. God is in our minds.

If one understands the teaching of Jesus, he or she knows God. The mind and Spirit are the same. When one is intelligent and well educated, he or she has great power.

If we do not develop our minds by learning truth, we are at the mercy of others. If we are ignorant and superstitious, we allow ourselves to be manipulated by those who are smarter than us. Truth is the only real authority and mental strength is the only real power. Those without knowledge or mental ability are at the mercy of others.

Good and evil are matters of choice. It is with the mind that we make choices. The choices we make determine the life we live. If one does not choose, someone else makes the decisions.

Living by faith is learning to know God and following Jesus or obeying God. Since God is all that is good, right, and true, and Jesus reveals God, we are saved from ignorance, superstition, and falsehood by following Jesus.

Real life is in the mind. We only live as conscious beings when our minds are working. When we are unconscious we do not commune with God.

When one is unable to think, one cannot be held responsible. Our responsibility is relative to our mental capability.

If we have intelligence we are capable of learning. The more intelligence one has, the greater one's capacity to learn. One is responsible according to one's intelligence and learning.

To enrich life, one must learn. The more one knows, the more truth one has and the more one's real authority. The more truth one has the less he or she is manipulated. The more nearly perfect one's knowledge of truth, the more faith one can exercise.

Jesus is known as The Great Teacher. His mission was to impart truth so that those who know him can live more abundantly.

Jesus was intelligent. He was probably of superior intelligence. When he was only a lad of twelve, he was capable of discussing important truths. We do not know what Jesus did from twelve to thirty, but we can be sure he acquired much knowledge and experience.

During Jesus' public ministry, he was never out-witted by others. He seems to have been better informed than any of his fellow human beings. He was regarded by all who knew him as The Teacher.

The last commandment of Jesus was, "Go and make learners or disciples." The only way we can be of lasting help is to teach people to think and learn. The more truth we learn the more real power we have. Truth is the authority. Jesus identifies with truth. The more truth we have the more like Jesus we are. When we know the truth about a subject, we are authorities on that subject.

When we are dealing with a subject that we know nothing about, we are dependent on others.

The Bread of Life and the Water of Life are the truths of God. God is the reality that makes life possible. The more truth we have the more closely we are united with God. When we have truth we know God. When we are deceived or ignorant, or superstitious, we do not know God. God is always the truth; he is never the falsehood or the evil.

When God gives us the Bread of Life or the Water of Life, he is sharing himself. God is Spirit. If we worship God, we worship him in Spirit and truth. We never worship the true God as an image or physical being. God is in the flesh but not of it. The life is in the blood. The blood feeds the mind. When the blood stops flowing the mind stops working. When the mind stops working we die. The body may live without the mind as a vegetable lives. No sensible person would try to communicate with or learn from a vegetable. We learn about mindless things but we do not learn from them. A teacher or learner has an active mind.

The Bread of Life and the Water of Life are mental foods. They are not given to the dead. No sensible person would give bread or water to a corpse.

To know truth is to live. To know Jesus is to know truth. To know Jesus as truth is to know God.

The righteous live by faith. The faithful live by truth. The faithful have the Bread of Life.

When we believe in Jesus we are saved from the deceitfulness of sin and we bear witness to truth. We need to share the Bread of Life.

The Light of the World

Which is better, to seek to justify ignorance or to overcome ignorance? Jesus teaches that he is determined to be a light rather than justify ignorance.

It is the Jesus way when we find a cure rather than try to justify an illness. It doesn't matter so much who sinned. What matters is overcoming sin. Why waste time blaming someone for what is wrong? Try to overcome the wrong rather than waste time and effort blaming.

If we believe in Jesus, we look for ways to enrich life. Why try to justify the status quo? No use cursing the dark—turn on the light!

We can easily blame the past generation for the ills of today, but what good would that do? "If it is to be it is up to me." My parents and their generation have lived their lives. I cannot change their lives. To blame my parents for my shortcomings is to waste the present. I cannot change those who have lived before me, but I can make a difference to those living now and those who will live later. God or reality is always in the present. The past is but a memory. The present is real. The future is only a hope or a dread.

If I am to enlighten anyone, I have to do it during my lifetime. The dead do not work. They decay. If we are dead in trespassing and sinning, we get more rotten day after day. The best way to treat the dead is to face reality and admit they are dead.

We cannot live our parents' lives, nor can we be our own children. We can glorify God or face reality by trying to cure the blind.

Jesus gives light. Like all good doctors, Jesus seeks to cure rather than to blame. Rather than seeking to blame others for the darkness, we are the light of our world. Which is better, to curse the parents or to help the children?

If you are blind, you need vision more than a lesson in history. Teaching history to the blind will not help them to see. It might help them to live with their blindness. Too often we help others to live with their ignorance. Jesus tells us to make learners. We are not to conserve the past, but to live in the present and build the Kingdom of God.

The way Jesus does is the best way we know. If we will follow him, we will go a long way toward restoring vision to the blind. If you believe Jesus is the light of the world you will do well to follow him.

Faith in god or facing reality is still the greatest need. When we find a blind person, we help by providing light more than sharing his or her darkness or ignorance.

When we quote Scripture instead of teaching truth, we share blindness. It isn't Adam's sin that matters. It is Jesus' light that we need. Instead of wasting time figuring how it got started; lets try to make improvement.

We will never redeem the world by conserving ignorance. We can redeem the world by applying truth. Jesus teaches what he has learned. Jesus teaches by example. He gives what he has to give. We have an opportunity to follow Jesus or to conserve ignorance. He tells us to go into all the world and make learners. Our mission is to teach truth. Teach people everywhere to face reality and enlighten the blind.

We do well to follow Jesus. It is better to ask, "What will make this right?" than to ask, "What caused this to be wrong?" The learners were interested in establishing blindness. Jesus was more interested in giving light.

If we look back to discuss blame, we are not fit for the Kingdom of Heaven. The road to Heaven lies ahead. If you want to reach Heaven, start where you are. You cannot live in the past. The response to the call of Jesus is not, "There I was," but "Here I am."

Jesus is the light of the world. We are his followers if we are the light of the world.

"Let your light so shine as to make God real to the world. In him is no darkness."

The Grace of God

The grace of God pertains to all that we receive freely from God. When we learn to think and act on our own without coercion from anyone we depend on the grace of God. When we learn that God is not partial and that his free gifts are available to all, we begin to live by faith.

We learn that every good gift and every perfect gift comes from God. We learn that God's gifts are available to each of us and that we receive them by faith. To live by faith is to think for ourselves and act according to our own thoughts. That means that we live by truth as God reveals truth to us.

To live by grace through faith is to resist manipulation, coercion, and falsehood. Instead of responding to rumors and propaganda without thinking, we think before we act. We live by faith in God not by fear of man. When we live by grace through faith we make the truth of God our Lord and not some lesser god.

God's grace is sufficient to supply all my needs. There is never a time when I cease to be responsible for my choices or behavior.

As I live by faith I prove over and over that God's truth is the only authority. I also learn that truth is reality. To face reality and obey the unchangeable laws of God is the way I profit from God's grace. When I do what I sincerely believe to be truth or Godly, I have a clear conscience and find favor with God. When I allow myself to be manipulated, coerced, or deceived, I am not approved by God.

To be approved by God we must live moral lives. Morality has to do with choosing what is good, right and true. Without choice there is no morality. The immoral person allows himself or herself to be manipulated or deceived into doing wrong instead of choosing to do right.

When we learn to think for ourselves, we learn that God is the source of all our blessings and that we receive God's blessings by grace - his being willing to give freely and through faith - our being willing and able to receive.

Jesus, whom we call the Saviour, Christ, or Messiah, reveals God to us. Jesus reveals God as truth or reality. There is no deception in God. God is all that we need for he is all that is good, right and true. We are deceived when we seek what is unreal or non-existent.

We express the truth of God by saying, "This is God's world or a real world." We are acting insanely when we refuse to accept truth or reality.

We are acting cowardly when we seek falsehoods rather than face truth. When we accept Jesus Christ as the embodiment or personification of truth, we are saved from ignorance, superstition, and other types of deception. We who accept Jesus as Lord accept truth or reality. To accept Jesus as truth is to reject Satan or deception.

Jesus tells us "Know the truth and the truth will set you free." Paul tells us, "God's grace is sufficient to supply all my needs."

It is a good thing for one to believe in reality or God. It is an evil thing for one to be deceived. The enemy of truth is deception by any name.

When we attribute worth to truth or when we worship God we live by grace through faith. When we live by faith we resist rumor, manipulations, coercion, and falsehood. We face the truth and accept the grace of God.

To worship God is to attribute worth to truth or reality. Thus the follower of Jesus worships the Lord God or attributes worth to truth. We celebrate worship with hymns, sincere meditations, testimonies, and other means of praise.

To attribute worth to anything deceptive or unreal is to engage in idolatry. Idolatry is the enemy of God. "Thou shalt worship or attribute worth to truth. Be not deceived." God's grace is sufficient. Have faith in God. Truth reigns.

The Godly Person

The Godly person has good will, lives right, learns truth, and does good.

The Godly person has a desire to learn, an open mind, and a ready hand.

The Godly person plans his work, works his plan, and does right.

The Godly person seeks energy, enthusiasm, and skill.

The Godly person is serious, consistent, and thorough.

The Godly person is single-minded, sane and, sensible.

The Godly person has love, compassion, and mercy.

The Godly person enlightens, encourages, and empowers.

The Godly person is without malice, prejudice, or ill will.

The Godly person learns from the past, lives in the present, and faces the future.

The Godly person has integrity, cooperates, and perseveres.

The Godly person acquires knowledge, understanding, and wisdom.

The Godly person works, rests, and restores.

The Godly person confesses, repents, and compensates.

The Godly person has open seeing eyes, listening ears, and a thinking mind.

The Godly person overcomes ignorance, superstition, and falsehood.

The Godly person respects others, protects the environment, and worships God.

The Godly person listens carefully, speaks truthfully, and acts wisely.

The Godly person grows physically, mentally, and socially.

The Godly person looks outward, forward, and upward.

The Godly person contrasts, compares, and completes.

The Godly person proves what is right, true, and good.

The Godly person seeks health, peace, and prosperity.

The Godly person seeks to avoid anger, confrontation, and strife.

The Godly person seeks to stay calm, cool, and confident.

The Godly person seeks, selects, and sows good seed.

The Godly person praises the true God who cares for us today, tomorrow, and forever.

Right with God

The person who believes that Jesus Christ is right with God and follows Jesus is right with God.

Jesus Christ is our example of good, righteousness and truth. Jesus consistently shows his love for us by his life and teaching. We show our love for Jesus by doing as he does. Jesus goes about doing good, speaking truth, and in all that he does and says, showing his love for humanity.

If we believe that Jesus came in the flesh and lived and died for the benefit of humanity, we are born of God and brothers or sisters of Jesus Christ. By our good will or Agape toward all humanity we show that we believe in Jesus Christ.

If we do not have Agape or good will toward all humanity, including our enemies, we do not believe in Jesus and we are yet sinners. Anyone who hates other people and would destroy them does not believe in Jesus.

Jesus came to save life not to destroy it. If we believe in Jesus we too try to save life. Agape or good will is the evidence of our believing in Jesus. If we believe in Jesus we have good will toward all people. We build God's Church or Kingdom by seeking to enrich the lives of all people.

Our mission is to help to reveal truth by showing good will toward all people and to make God known by showing good will and living so as to enrich the lives of all concerned.

God is love. Love does not do evil. If we love, we help. Love in action is mutual helpfulness. It consists of doing good, living right and being truthful. God is God of all. God expresses himself through his unchangeable laws that control the universe. Everything that works for the benefit of humanity is in harmony with God's laws. Everything that that harms humanity is against God's laws. We are right with God to the extent that we show our love for all people. We are wrong when we show partiality and mistreat people. The love of God is impartial. God loves, or God is love. God is love, truth and right. God is eternal. He is present and he never changes. We serve God when we help humanity. We love God to the extent that we love all humanity.

If we do not love all people to the extent that we have good will toward all, we do not love God. If we hate anybody we need to repent. Unless we repent we will perish. To perish is to be separated from God. To be separated from God is to die spiritually or mentally. When we have no love for humanity we are spiritually dead. One who is completely selfish is without love. One who is selfish is dead in trespasses and sins. When one believes in Jesus, he loves humanity. Love for enemies is evidence that one believes in Jesus.

The lust of the flesh, the lust of the eye, and the pride of life are the ways of the worldly who do not believe in Jesus. Lust and pride are indications of selfishness as opposed to love. If we live for self only, we are immature and incomplete. We have not passed from death unto life. We have not been born from above. Selfish people are not builders of the Kingdom of God.

To be a disciple of Jesus is to move toward maturity. It is to deny self and seek the benefit of all. It is to become a servant of God. Becoming like Jesus is overcoming selfishness and being motivated by good will.

Being right with God is being right with humanity. Loving God is loving humanity. Loving humanity is believing in Jesus Christ. You cannot study the life of Jesus without studying about his life on earth. If you do not believe that he lived in the flesh, you do not believe in Jesus at all. If you believe that Jesus lived, you have to believe that he loved. The life of Jesus is the manifestation of the love of God. Jesus shows us how to overcome ignorance, superstition, falsehood, and ill will. Jesus gives us the formula for success in life, "Love your neighbors as yourself and do unto others as you would have them do unto you." "I am the way, the truth and the life. No one comes to be right with God who does not believe in me," so said Jesus. Have faith in God, believe in Jesus Christ.

The Reign of God

How can we bring about the reign of God? In what sense does God reign already? What is my role in bringing about the reign of God?

The reign of God is the rule or dominion of God in the life of an individual. As each person submits to God's will and unites with others who have submitted to his will, God's Kingdom grows. God's Kingdom will continue growing until it encompasses the whole earth. Every person will submit to God's rule or perish. Those who believe in Jesus Christ will become members of God's Kingdom. Those who reject truth as presented by Jesus Christ will die in their sins or perish.

The Kingdom of God is made up of people who love one another.

People who love one another work together for mutual benefit. They obey the laws of God and dwell in peace. God's love or good will brings people together. The righteous live by faith in a true, righteous, and loving God.

God reigns already in the sense that his laws govern life on earth and elsewhere. The person who obeys God's laws is saved from all the curses of disobedience and receives all the blessings of obedience. God rules all people by his laws. God rules the citizens of his Kingdom by his grace.

The grace of God is his gift to humanity. All we need or desire is available when we exercise faith in God. When we obey God's laws that control the earth, we live in harmony with truth. When we are in harmony with truth all things work together for our benefit. When we work against truth or reality all things work against us. Unless we repent and face reality we perish.

The goal of the church or body of Christ is to bring everybody into the Kingdom of Righteousness. If we believe in Jesus Christ and follow him, we become peacemakers and are called children of God. As children of God we love one another and promote what is good. As we work together for good we bring about the reign of God. When we work against good we promote the destructive forces and in doing so destroy others and ourselves. If we submit to God's will and obey his eternal and unchangeable laws we live. If we rebel against God we perish.

When we seek god's grace and love one another as Jesus loves us we overcome ignorance, superstition, falsehood and ill will and learn to experience fellowship, joy and peace. When we experience true fellowship, joy and peace we live after the Spirit and in harmony with God. When we choose to live after the flesh we destroy ourselves. "The lust of the flesh, the lust of the eye, and the pride of life are at enmity with God." Worldly lusts keep us from the grace of God. When we refuse God's love, we cannot accept his grace. If we choose to reject the gifts of God, we choose to perish. God is love. His kingdom is built on love. Love seeks to help others. The kingdoms of the flesh are built on lusts. The worldly-minded, self-destructing people destroy themselves by trying to exploit others. Life is reciprocal.

What one wants is received when that one seeks to give it to others. We receive from God what we give to others. God takes away from us what we would take away from others.

Real life is achieved by our giving out. Death comes from our always taking in. Waters of life flow.

One who does not give to help others is like the Dead Sea. The Kingdom of God is a kingdom of grace. God gives us what we need when we give to others what they need. We are truly saved from selfishness by grace through faith.

God gives us his best when we give our best. We give to God when we help to meet human need. We destroy ourselves when we practice human greed.

God's reign will be complete when all people everywhere learn to love one another. Jesus is our Lord and Saviour. The commandment is "Love one another as I love you." Greater love has no one. He gave his life. He revealed God. God is love. God's love saves us. Let God reign - love one another.

The Gospel of Christ

The Gospel of Christ is the good news that God loves all people and that it is God's will for us to be united in bonds of peace.

Gospel or good news is the proclamation that God is no respecter of persons. God's people are those who are peacemakers without malice but with liberty and justice for all.

The Gospel of Christ is the message of the love or good will of God toward all people everywhere at all times.

Those who accept the Gospel of Christ do all in their power to promote peace and unity.

Those who believe in Jesus Christ believe in unity and promote peace. Those who preach the Gospel are ambassadors of good will. Those who believe in Jesus believe in one God, one humanity, one faith, one baptism.

Those who hear the Gospel and accept Christ as Lord and Saviour are born of God. As peacemakers they become children of God.

When we hear and respond to the unifying good news, we love our neighbors as ourselves. Our former enemies become friends. We are no longer Jews and Samaritans, male and female, bond and free; we are henceforth "one nation under God with a new birth of freedom."

The Gospel or Good News is the message of salvation. It is the truth of God that overcomes prejudice, malice, ignorance, superstition, falsehood and ill will. It removes the necessity for war and unites us in bonds of peace.

The Spirit of God is a Spirit of Unity. When we accept Christ by accepting the message of peace and good will, we become a fellowship of sharing.

The Gospel of Christ is the basis for true prosperity for all. When we accept Christ we begin to look for ways and means of enriching lives.

The Gospel of Christ reveals God as he is. God is love. God is truth. God is just. God is good. God is present. God is perfect. God is the Father of all who would live in peace.

The Gospel of Christ promotes health, wealth, and wisdom.

Those who accept Christ as Lord of all desire salvation for all.

Those who hear and believe the Gospel of Christ are set free. They are no longer in bondage to sin. Having become children of God we begin to pursue truth and love. We want to know what is good and right for all humanity. By hearing and proclaiming the Gospel of Christ we become instruments of God's peace.

The Gospel of Christ or Good News is being proclaimed by people of good will of many cultures, nations and languages.

The Gospel of Christ is the message of salvation. It is the true revelation of God. It is our means of glorifying God. To glorify God is to make God known. To make God known is the mission of all people who believe in Jesus the Christ. The scriptures teach us that "whether we eat or drink or whatever we do we should make God known or glorify God." Paul, the Apostle, said, "Woe is me if I preach not the Gospel."

When we preach the Gospel we are spreading good news and promoting health, peace, wisdom, and prosperity so as to enrich the lives of all people everywhere.

When we neglect to preach the Gospel we are allowing the forces of falsehood and division to thrive in the world.

The Apostle Paul was willing to suffer many kinds of hardship as he preached or proclaimed the Gospel of Christ. He considered the Gospel of first importance. Compared to the Gospel of Christ other things were as garbage or refuse. What was true for Paul should be true for each of us.

It is written, "The Righteous shall live by faith." Faith in God comes by hearing. We have faith in God because we have heard the Gospel of Christ. If we have heard the Gospel of Christ, we know that God is our God. All there is is available to us when we have faith in God. God loves each and every one of us. What he has done for others he will do for you.

Yes, the Gospel is Good News.

The Kingdom of God (I)

The Kingdom of God is the reign of God. It is made up of those who follow Jesus as Lord.

The Kingdom or reign of God is a growing Kingdom. It begins in one's life as a small seed and ultimately, has complete control.

The Kingdom or rule of God is the blissful condition that exists when all is in harmony. When all jealousy and strife are done away with, wherever Jesus is Lord, there is the Kingdom of God.

Everyone who accepts Jesus as Lord and follows his teaching is a citizen of God's Kingdom.

When Jesus becomes one's Lord, that person will die for what he or she believes in. When one makes that kind of commitment, his life harmonizes. When one is living in harmony with all people and all things, he or she is experiencing the Kingdom of God.

The Kingdom of God takes priority over all else. Life in God's Kingdom is living by faith. When one lives by faith in God as he is revealed through Jesus Christ, he or she obeys the laws of God and overcomes all conflict.

The Kingdom or rule of God influences all of life. It is like leaven. When one is living in obedience to Christ, he or she is not manipulated or tossed about by every wind of doctrine. That person has a sense of security and an attitude of love. When one believes in Christ, he or she has a sense of direction and purpose. Living by faith is having a goal to move towards. It is having an anchor to hold one in place. It is having a handle to hold on to.

The Kingdom of God is more than law and works. One may obey the law out of fear. One may do good works for gain. One believes in Christ because of truth. One accepts truth because of his or her integrity. When one is committed to doing right, he or she does what he or she believes to be right.

Those outside God's Kingdom are evil. They do not follow Jesus. They do not live by faith. To be legalistic or to do good for selfish reasons is to be outside the will of God.

It is God's will that we choose to do right even if we have to suffer for doing so. If we have faith in Christ, we choose to obey the laws of God out of a sense of love rather than obligation or duty. When we love who we are, what we do, and with whom we associate or relate to, we are having a blissful experience. When we have a blissful experience, we are in the will of God.

Being in God's Kingdom means we are not guilty of willful wrongdoing. It means we choose to do what we are doing. It means we are willing to die for what we believe in. It means we are living by faith in Jesus Christ.

All who believe in Jesus, as God's revelation of himself, are born into his Kingdom. No one is excluded. Anyone may enter God's Kingdom by dying to evil, by accepting Christ. When one gives up legalism and the idea of working for reward and chooses to live by faith, that one isn't far from the Kingdom. Sooner or later everyone will either believe in Christ or perish. All who choose Christ will live forever.

Jesus teaches us that many who are first to know what is right will be last to choose what is right. Those without prejudice will enter first. Little children will enter ahead of the teachers of the law. The prejudiced selfish Pharisees will be the last to enter.

It is not the warlords who kill the enemy or the rich who buy off the enemy that enter the Kingdom of God. It is the humble who love the enemy and want to redeem them that enter the Kingdom.

The Kingdom of God is the will of God for all humanity. When we are in God and God is in us, we live in harmony with all God's creation. We know who we are and where we are going. We love everybody and we accept everybody with love. We believe in one God and one people.

When we are in God's will, we are willing to suffer rather than do evil. We do not ask, "Is it easy?"–we ask, "Is it right?" We purpose in our hearts to do what is good, what is right, and what is true. We trust God and follow Jesus. Whatever pleases God is what we desire. We know that we always need more faith. We walk by faith. "Thy Kingdom come. Thy will be done."

The Way of the Lord (2)

As for me, Jesus Christ is Lord. I value the teaching and example of Jesus. Jesus shows us that intelligence, intuition, good will, and common sense coupled with love, mercy, justice, and compassion take precedence over the Law of Moses.

The law ruled until John the Baptizer. Until John, people of Israel depended on the law for salvation. They did not believe anything justified breaking the law. They did not recognize the validity of repentance. Jesus said of the Pharisees that they were so legalistic that, "Heaven and Earth may pass, but not one jot or tittle of the law can be changed." They put the law above human welfare. Most of the controversy between Jesus and the Pharisees was about the letter or literal interpretation of the Law. They were like the Fundamentalists of our day. Their view was, "The law says it; I believe it; that settles it."

John, and later Jesus, came preaching repentance and for-giveness. Jesus believed that the Sabbath was made for man, not man for the Sabbath. Jesus used the observance of the

Sabbath as an example of the law. The law is to be used for the benefit of man.

Jesus teaches us to do what is beneficial to human beings, even if it involves going against some technicality of the law.

Jesus would say, "Live by the principles of the law, not by the letter of the law." It is not against the principles of the law to do good on the Sabbath or any other time.

Jesus teaches us to acquire knowledge, understanding, and wisdom. Having acquired knowledge, understanding, and wisdom, we are to have good will and use our judgement and common sense when making decisions. We are to make decisions that are helpful and not harmful to other human beings.

If we make mistakes, we are to repent or correct the mistakes. Instead of being legalistic or literal we are to seek a benefit. We can always observe the intent or principles of the law. We cannot always observe the technicalities without sometimes doing harm.

The legalistic Jews or Israelites would swear to their own hurt. Jesus considered such oaths as foolish. He teaches us that it is better not to take such oaths. Never keep a foolish promise when it will cause you to harm someone. Use common sense and good will.

Jesus upheld the law, but he insisted on using good will and good sense in obeying it. If one insists on obeying the law to the letter, he may be right but end up dead.

Jesus never upholds rigid thinking. Good will and good sense demand flexibility. Sometimes we fell oaks and crush rocks. Wisdom is better than foolishness.

Jesus would say, "Stick to tradition and custom so long as they do not hinder advancement of God's Kingdom or God's will. But seek first the Kingdom of God and his righteousness."

Jesus opens Scriptures to us if we have open eyes, open ears, and an open mind. But Jesus tells us to repent when wrong. He tells us to compromise and negotiate when it is wise to do so.

If you profess to follow Jesus, you need to know what Jesus teaches. Jesus teaches good will toward all people. He loves even his enemies. If we believe in Jesus, we trust God's grace. We know that the law does not save. It is always God's will for us to be helpful and not harmful. If you follow Jesus you will live by faith. To live by faith is to trust in the providence of God. "The Bible says" is meaningless if you interpret it literally. When you say, "The Bible says..." you need to know what the Bible says. Jesus opens the Bible. Some of our Fundamentalist preachers offer it to us closed. Do you follow Jesus or the Pharisees? Whose interpretation of the law do you believe and follow? As for me, I believe in Jesus. I believe in compromise, negotiation, and common sense when they work for the benefit of humanity.

I believe in the Spirit of the law. I choose life. "The letter or literalism kills. The Spirit of good will and common sense gives life."

The Day of Salvation

The day of salvation is always the present. Eternity is now. We cannot postpone the passing of time. You cannot live yesterday or tomorrow. You can only live in the present. Yesterday is gone. Tomorrow has not arrived. You live now.

The opportunity for Dives to help Lazarus was while they were both living. When Lazarus was gone, it was too late for Dives to help him or for him to help Dives. Death separates us from one another. We die as we live. Once we are dead, our day of helping one another is gone. If we could live our lives over under the same circumstances we would live them the same way. God does not change his laws. They are the same always. We have Moses and the other prophets. If we do not hear them, we would not hear another. Truth is truth. If we refuse truth when we know truth, we refuse it no matter the source.

We choose to do right or wrong. We decide. Decisions are made by the one who receives a message, not by the one who delivers it. The messenger has the responsibility to deliver the message. The one who receives the message takes it from there. If one is dead, he or she cannot be helped. We can only help one another while we are living. "This is the day of salvation." In his day means while he was alive.

We are to work while it is our day. The time is coming when our lives will be over. When we die we will be separated from the living. We cannot help the dead. The dead cannot help us. Death is a gulf between the individuals that would serve one another. It is the darkness that comes at the end of the day. There is no value in trying to live in the past. Yesterday is gone forever. There is no value in trying to live tomorrow. Tomorrow has not come. "This is the day the Lord has made." If I am wise I will rejoice and be glad today while I am living. Our mission is to glorify God. God is the God of the living. He will always be the God of the living.

God is eternal. Eternity is now. God gives eternal life. We live now. We either help one another now or never. We can learn from the past but we cannot live in it. We can prepare for the future but we cannot live in the future.

Wishful thinking gets us nowhere. We reap what we sow, not what we wish we had sown. We live by faith. We do not live by wish. By faith we seek what we hope for. By faith we move toward our goals. Faith is power. A wish is but a passing fancy. Faith changes things. Wishes do nothing.

Wishes are like excuses. They serve us when we do nothing. We have learned that "idleness is the devil's workshop." The devil is whatever keeps us from serving one another. If we remember when we are dead, we will rejoice in what good we have done, or we will regret doing nothing good. We will think of those whom we have helped or those who could have helped us.

If we have brothers, they too will have to live now. God will not change to accommodate anyone. You cannot accept Christ yesterday or tomorrow. This is your life. You cannot live another person's life. This is your day. You cannot live in another time.

The righteous face reality. They live by faith in the living God who is the same yesterday, today, and forever. Jesus, as the revelation of God, is also the same. The same Jesus whom you see go away is the one who will return. We cannot change God. We are the ones who must change. Any changes we make will be while we are living. In the grave we do not act. It is not a place for work, but a place for rest. The grave is a lonely place.

We love one another while we live. We live by faith.

The Kingdom of God (2)

The Kingdom of God is among us. It is not something or some place which we enter or go to. The Kingdom of God is the reign of God or the will of God.

This earth where we are is the place where we live. Now is the time in which we live. If we believe in Jesus as the revelation of a perfect God and live by faith in the God whom he reveals, we become citizens of God's Kingdom.

The Kingdom of God is in the world but not of it. We attain the Kingdom by living like Jesus. We are born into the Kingdom by accepting Jesus as Lord. God gives the Kingdom in exchange for our faith in him. Thus we are saved by grace through faith.

When we are saved by grace, God's free gift, through faith, our accepting personally the revelation of God through Jesus Christ, we become citizens of God's Kingdom. As citizens of God's Kingdom, we live by faith in God.

Our mission as citizens of God's Kingdom is to please God by overcoming the sins of the world. God's Kingdom is that state of perfect bliss where there is peace and prosperity similar to what Israel experienced during the reign of Solomon. The difference is that the kingdom of Solomon was a literal kingdom of riches and peace encompassing all Israel. The kingdom of Israel under Solomon was what seemed to be a perfect kingdom. The desire of the leader, Solomon, was to emphasize serving the Lord God and to make him the center of the kingdom. As long as Solomon accomplished his purpose, his kingdom or rule seemed to be ideal. All the countries or leaders that knew about Solomon recognized his wisdom and achievements. He was respected by all who knew him.

The Kingdom of God is similar to the kingdom of Solomon. It is founded by Jesus Christ and has the marks of an ideal Kingdom. The citizens of God's Kingdom live in peace and enjoy the gifts of God. They live by faith. They are in the world but not of it.

So far as the territory was concerned, Solomon did not change the location of his kingdom. The difference was in the way people, under Solomon, lived. The same is true of the Kingdom of God. It is not somewhere beyond this world. The Kingdom is here and now. It is a Kingdom of people who live by faith in God rather than following the crowds around us.

The Kingdom of God is not a different area, but a different way of life. The citizens of God's Kingdom live by faith not by sight but insight. If we live by faith we do not seek to escape to some perfect place, we seek to transform the place where we are. Like Abraham of old, we seek a Kingdom whose builder and maker is God. It is by faith in God that we live in his Kingdom.

When we are born from above, we begin to seek, as our first priority, the Kingdom of God and his righteousness. We renounce our loyalty to the ways of the world around us. We no longer follow the crowds, but seek to do the will of God. We do not seek to find a place where all is well. We seek to make all well where we are.

If we study the prayer of Jesus, we find that he does not take us out of this age, but seeks to keep us from evil. The Kingdom of God is in our midst. We enter the Kingdom by faith in God and we live by faith. We worship God as he reveals himself to us through Jesus Christ and his followers. God will reward us according to our own faith. Without faith we receive nothing from God.

My Sin

What is my sin? My sin is whatever I think, say or do that is contrary to the laws of God. Whatever I do that shows a lack of faith in a holy, righteous, and just God is sin.

My sin is personal. It is what separates me as an individual from the approval of God. It is my coming up short or missing the mark in life.

My sin is not doing what I ought to do, or my doing what I ought not do. My sin is indifference, neglect, or doing wrong.

My sin is not maturing as I ought to mature. It is not living a balanced life. It is putting too much emphasis on some things and not enough emphasis on other things.

My sin is not accepting the gifts of God. It is my having too much pride to receive and not being humble enough to learn.

My sin is not learning what I need to know, not trying to understand my relationship with others, and not seeking wisdom from God through others.

My sin is allowing myself to follow superstitions rather than seeking to prove what is right and wholesome.

My sin is choosing falsehood rather than reality. It is in not seeking truth for fear the truth might cause pain and suffering.

My sin is procrastination. It is not doing what needs to be done when it needs to be done.

My sin is blaming others for my mistakes rather than practicing self-discipline.

My sin is talking when I should be listening. It is being foolish when I should be gaining wisdom.

My sin is trying to judge others when I should be examining myself.

My sin is not having vision enough to prevent trouble and accidents. Thus having to spend time correcting mistakes.

My sin is not counting the cost before doing the project or taking the journey.

My sin is confusing lust with love, and friendship with affection.

My sin is following in the wrong direction when I should be leading in the right direction.

My sin is flattering the mediocre when I should be commending the good.

My sin is hurriedly building on the sand when I should be building on a rock.

My sin is walking by sight rather than living by faith.

My sin is allowing myself to be manipulated rather than making decisions.

My sin is giving to the greedy when I should be giving to the needy.

My sin is trying to be seen when I should be observing.

My sin is not being what I want others to be and not doing what I want others to do.

My sin is fretting about evil when I should be enjoying good.

My sin is yielding to all kinds of temptations of this age instead of choosing only what is good.

My sin is not living every day in every way so as to let others see that I have been with Jesus and in so living be a revelation of a God who can and will deliver us from evil and supply for our needs.

My sin is what keeps me from perfect fellowship with God and my fellow beings.

May the eternal, loving, ever present, Holy, righteous, and true God forgive me of all my sin and help me live a more abundant life.

The Truth

The truth is the word of God or the law of God. The truth is reality or what is. Jesus upholds the law of God. He faces reality.

Faith to Jesus is knowing and facing reality with all the wisdom one can attain. It is never bowing to falsehood.

God is whatever is true or real. No matter what the circumstances it is always best to face the truth. Truth is always God or God's word. True prophets always face truth. There is no way for one to be faithful to God and propagate lies. Telling a lie over and over does not make it truth.

No one can follow Jesus of Nazareth without facing truth.

The opposite of truth is falsehood. The devil or Satan is the personification of falsehood. Anyone who always faces truth is of God. Anyone who does not face truth is of the devil. True religions or people who have true convictions are groups of people who are loyal to what they believe is truth.

False religions, or people who do not seek truth, are made up of people like the Pharisees who are hypocritical. They pretend to have truth, but are following traditions of men. Bible quoters who never think through what they are quoting are following traditions. There seems to be many people who would rather be wrong than to be real. Instead of seeking God or truth, they quote what someone of old has said.

Think of all the strife in the world that is caused by falsehood. In order to gain or retain power, people and nations of people spread propaganda. Adolph Hitler was a master of propaganda. He would say the same lie over and over until naive people believe him. He was able to deceive whole nations of people.

All warmongers are followers of Satan. All nations who are willing to kill to uphold their traditions are Satanic.

Jesus Christ upholds truth. He emphasizes his belief in truth by saying, "Not one little bit of reality can be changed." He says, "If it were possible for Heaven and Earth to pass away truth would still stand." There is no way to change reality. You can accept or reject the teaching about reality, but you cannot change reality. The word is cannot be modified or changed. It is never right to say iser. Like the word perfect, is cannot be modified. Something can be more nearly perfect, but it cannot be more perfect.

When we say be perfect we mean be right and complete. Only God is always right and complete because God is the reality. It doesn't matter how smart one is, he cannot change reality.

The prophets learned what was real and tried to teach it to others. They learned the law of cause and effect. They could tell by the trends what was coming.

We say that something mankind cannot control is an act of providence or God. If it is real and we cannot understand or control it, we say it is providential.

It is natural, means man has not changed or added to it or taken away from it.

When a religion propagates lies they are false and wrong. When they bear witness to truth they are following Jesus. Jesus is the person or personification of truth. He is the way to live. True power that lasts is always based on truth. No authority that is not real is going to stand permanently.

It is right to look for a Kingdom whose builder and maker is god. We need to try to know the truth about anything we act upon. If anything is worth doing, it is always better when done right. If we sin or do wrong, we have to bear the consequence.

A righteous person or one who believes in Jesus Christ tries to do right. If he or she makes a mistake, he or she repents or bears the consequence. "You cannot do wrong and be right at the same time."

All education is concerned with truth. People who indoctrinate may be concerned with truth or tradition. Cults are all more concerned with propaganda than truth. A cult has some leader that tells the followers what to do. People of faith think before they act.

The main emphasis of Jesus is to know truth. "If we learn to be true to ourselves we cannot be false to others." Jesus personifies truth and good will. You cannot have good will or Agape love and be a liar. All liars are unfaithful. "Without faith it is impossible to please God."

If you want to be right with God, you want to know truth. If you are not willing to uphold truth, you are yet in your sins.

The result of sin is death to integrity. Sin enslaves. It punishes. It kills. "Believe in Jesus Christ and be saved." Know the truth. Be free.

Israel

The Kingdom of Israel is not the Kingdom of God. It is a type of kingdom, but not a type that is adequate for modern man. Ancient Israel is, perhaps, the realistic kingdom for that day. But mankind has had thousands of years in which to improve.

God is reality. God's Kingdom must be a Kingdom of reality. A primitive people are a primitive people. They are like an infant compared to a more mature people.

Look at the differences between Israel and the primitive people in Palestine when the tribes of Moses returned. The native people were still full of superstitions. They were so stupid that they bowed to idols that they themselves had made. They even thought having sex would influence crops. They believed that sacrificing their best would appease God as though an idol could do something for them.

The man Abraham, began to reason and determined that such idolatry was utter foolishness. He had enough intelligence to reason that truth or reality prevails and that superstitions are signs of ignorance.

Abraham came to believe that he and his descendants could do better. He could visualize a better civilization. Like any thinking person, Abraham broke with tradition and used his own intelligence.

When people are too stupid to think or too immature to do anything worthwhile, they look for outside authority. When they think, they begin to observe what is true and what is false.

God is truth or the personification of truth. The devil or Satan came to personify what is false. Abraham and others like him choose truth or reality. They are unwilling to believe that inanimate things or changing things that are without intelligence should be bowed to. Because the people of Israel chose to face reality, we say they were people of God or God's Chosen People.

As the followers of Abraham saw that there is more to be gained by being realistic than by being stupid or foolish enough to bow to idols, they began to prosper or be blessed. As they faced reality they were opposed by the stupid and foolish. By fighting or acting with more intelligence, they were able to overcome opposition. They soon began to worship or attribute worth to reality. They made distinctions or observed what worked and what didn't. Each family taught their children what they had learned and encouraged them to be realistic.

To be realistic we have to recognize change and make progress. We have to build on truth and act on faith. The important thing is faith. We must believe that the future will be better if we keep on learning truth and applying it to help ourselves and others. By learning and applying truth and fighting against idolatry, the people whom we call Israel became a progressive people. They learned that in order to make progress and face reality, they had to separate themselves from the people who worshipped idols or acted foolishly.

The Israelites made progress when they lived like Abraham by proving what was real and practicing what they learned. They had foolish wars and foolish rituals when they drifted back into idolatry.

When people worship God or attribute worth to truth, they make progress and feel good about themselves. When people refuse to think or lack courage to face reality, they seek external authority. When people do not trust reality or truth, which we call God, they follow living or dead dictators. When people follow strong men of the present rather than thinking and seeking God or reality and working together, they are allowing external authority to control them. When they blindly follow traditions they are being foolish.

The Lord Jesus teaches us to learn to think, to prove all things, and to hold to what is good. If we do this we will be saved from the foolishness of falsehood. By being realistic and seeking truth we will live more abundant lives.

When we teach truth and practice truth we learn to live in peace and enjoy life. Any well-informed and disciplined people know that life that is real is better than life that is based on falsehood.

Jesus of Nazareth was an intelligent and well-informed person of good will. He faced reality rather then falsehood, even unto death. He taught us the value of truth by living it to the end of his life. To follow Jesus is to learn and to live. It is to choose truth and face reality with good will toward all people.

If we have the faith of Abraham and follow Jesus we will live.

Prayer (I)

Prayer is not expressing preferences and making wishes.

Prayer is mediation, study, thinking, desiring, planning, seriously doing, and showing gratitude. It is seriously seeking and applying truth so as to help living creatures, especially fellow humans beings, to get more out of life.

Prayer is not quoting what some have said or talking to some imaginary being or imaginary God. Nor is it making requests of some idol.

To pray without ceasing is to always seek to be good, righteous, and true. It is to also encourage others to be good, righteous, and true.

When Jesus says, "there is none good but God," he means that

God is the only one that is perfectly Good. God is the goal we move toward. We can only be worthy of eternal life or Godly life, when we give all we are and all we have toward becoming perfect.

God is perfection in every sense of the word. We cannot improve on perfection. A rich person may obey all the law, but unless his Heart which means all of him is right, he is not going to inherit the state of eternal of Godly life.

Money is a medium of exchange. It is not good to hoard money when you have more than enough and live among people who have less than enough. Being moral does not make one perfect. Perfection involves relationships. When we reach perfection by giving all we are and all we have, we can sit down with God. If we follow Jesus that is what we seek after.

God is perfect in love, justice, mercy, power, and all other ways. God is the concept of perfection.

When anything, any person, any concept, any condition is perfect, it is Godly. When anything, any person, any concept, any condition is imperfect, it needs to be improved or made better.

We take pride in what is perfect for the purpose for which it is intended. If it isn't perfect for the purpose or use intended, it needs to be improved.

If we make something or do something that isn't good enough to fulfill the purpose or use intended, we say it is lacking.

Progressive people are constantly trying to do better or make better or more useful things. We should never stop and boast. We can always do more or better.

When we have done our best, we still haven't anything to boast about. We can never be better than perfect. The proud try to get credit for what they have done. The humble keep on learning and improving. The humble are those who seek perfection. The proud seek attention.

The proud are hypocrites or play actors. They try to draw attention to themselves. They are not worshippers of God. They worship themselves. If we are humble, we are more likely to speak well of others. When we speak well of others, we promote goodness. Those whom we speak well of are encouraged or their reputation is enhanced. When we think only of ourselves, we become conceited bigots and a drag on society. It were better that we had not been born. "He or she is proud" is never a compliment. "He or she is humble" is always a compliment.

The proud resist God; the humble seek God. Perfection or God is the goal of life. The proud try to appear God. There can be only one God; the proud is not it. The proud is always immature. The proud to others is like having to eat a fruit that has been pulled green.

The humble are a praying people. They are constantly seeking to be more useful. The humble move toward perfection. The proud act as though they had attained perfection. The proud talk; the humble listen. The proud are foolish; the humble are wise. The proud are like the Pharisees; the humble are like Jesus. The proud are living in mansions while they build huts for others; the humble live in huts while they build mansions for others. Life is reciprocal.

Pray without ceasing. Remain humble.

The Flesh and the Spirit

The Flesh is the lower or physical nature of human beings or any intelligent being. It is not mind controlling matter. When we think through what we are doing and choose what is good, righteous, and true and, thus, enhance life for everyone concerned, we are obeying the Spirit. When we do foolish things just to feel good at the moment with no regard for doing good, being righteous, and facing reality we are living after the Flesh.

Another difference in the Flesh and Spirit is, the one who lives after the Flesh lets others manipulate or follows the crowd or takes the path of least resistance.

The person who is led by the Spirit counts the cost and does what enhances life for all concerned whether he feels like doing it or not. In simple language, the Spirit led person is committed to showing good will or love or enhancing life for all people. The Flesh led person does what feels good at the moment whether it is helpful or not. The Spirit led person is wise. The Flesh led person is foolish.

With the exception of things over which we have no control all we do that is harmful is of the flesh or of ill will. A person who Agape loves or as we say has good will, refuses to harm himself or others. A Spirit led person lives by faith. He or she tries to prove all things and hold to what is helpful and not harmful. Such a person does not like manipulation by others, nor does he or she follow the crowd.

The Spirit is from within. It is the mind of the living being controlling his or her desires so as to be helpful in enhancing life.

The Spirit led person does what is best for all concerned rather than living by feelings or emotions. The Spirit led person has emotions, but controls his or her emotions. We speak of such a person as one who has good will and self-control.

The emotion led or fleshly controlled person does what feels good. Their lives are inconsistent and foolish and at times, dangerous or harmful.

A follower of Jesus Christ studies to learn truth and then practices self-control and good will.

Jesus is an example of a Spirit led person. Jesus thought for himself and practiced self-control and showed good will. Jesus had temptations, but he was led by the Spirit and not the flesh. If you follow Jesus, you will never go wrong. Jesus is our best example.

If you are led by the Spirit you think and plan and use wisdom. If you are led by the flesh you act childish and let others dominate you or let your own feelings dominate you. Without self-control you are a slave either to others or to your emotions.

What each person needs is faith in reality or truth, which we call God. "All things work together for good when we face reality or truth with good will and self-control." All things work toward evil to those who accept falsehood and show ill will.

Truth and/or reality is Godly. Falsehood and indifference are Satanic. It is true that the righteous—those who relate properly to others, live by faith. Those who do not live by faith allow themselves to be manipulated by external authority or their own emotions or feelings. They who do wrong are lacking faith. They are not freed by truth and good will. When we know truth we have good will or Agape—the basis of life. Truth is what is. False is what is not. Truth is positive. False is negative. Truth is for. False is against. Truth leads to life. False leads to death.

When we educate people, we teach them to think and live by the mind. Education is a maturation experience. Only an educated person can live by the Spirit instead of the flesh. An educated person with good will does what he or she believes is best for all concerned. He or she is a free being. He or she has learned that our enemies are our own ignorance, superstitions, falsehoods, and all else that enslaves. A Spirit led person enhances life.

Sin (2)

When we allow our emotions to control us instead of our minds we lack self-control. When we lack self-control we resort to pleasure and selfishness. Instead of doing what is helpful for all concerned the emotional person does what makes he or she feel good at the moment.

Living right means being kind and considerate and doing what is fair. To follow Jesus is to do unto others what one desires for oneself. The follower of Jesus has a feeling of equality. To be Christ-like is to do what one knows or believes to be best for all concerned.

For the follower of Jesus obeying the laws of God or being realistic is working for all concerned. The follower of Jesus desires to be at peace with all people and to see all people prosper. It hurts a follower of Jesus just as much to cause another to suffer as to cause oneself to suffer. The follower of Jesus keeps his promises or observes provisions of contracts. The follower of Jesus tries to correct what is wrong.

The follower of Jesus does not belittle anyone. It is the will of the follower of Jesus that everyone grow in grace and in knowledge, understanding, and wisdom.

The follower of Jesus repents of mistakes as soon as he or she realizes they have hurt or harmed someone by action or neglect.

The follower of Jesus never deliberately harms another, even one's enemies.

"The one who knows he or she should help someone and does not help is committing sin."

Sin is not looking for opportunities to be helpful to others.

Sin is being proud of what one has said or done that provokes jealousy or shows envy.

Sin is showing desire for pleasure more than fellowship or mutual love.

Sin is competing to destroy rather than to build up.

Sin is seeking to destroy enemies rather than seeking to make friends.

Sin is saying or doing anything that is harmful or destructive to others, including one's enemies.

Sin is acting falsely instead of being truthful.

Sin is being unreal instead of real.

Sin is not facing reality but acting on some phobia, falsehood, superstition, or ill will.

Sin is trying to believe a lie or trying to do the impossible or dangerous.

Sin is seeking a sign or miracle instead of seeking truth.

Sin is seeking to set boundaries rather than to make progress.

Sin is seeking to control others rather than to control oneself.

Sin is rebelling against authorized authority.

Sin is working against decency and order.

Sin is postponing or procrastinating rather than making use of time.

Sin is missing the purpose or mark.

Sin is to worship any kind of an idol; be it a thing, a ritual, or some foolishness.

Sin is anything that needs to be corrected being continued without correction.

Sin is not planning ahead or discerning trends and thus allowing evil or negativism in one's life.

Sin is judging others instead of being a good example.

Sin is living a shallow life.

The Jesus We Worship

Jesus of Nazareth was born in humble surroundings; but of great parents who descended from distinguished characters. Every one of Jesus' forebears or ancestors was outstanding for having made some notable contribution to human welfare.

Very early in life, Jesus learned self-discipline. By the time he was twelve years old, Jesus was discussing important topics, at times, with scholarly people.

It is likely that he applied himself to learning every day. When he began his public ministry, he was far ahead of his peers. What had become common knowledge to Jesus seemed like miracles to the masses.

All of us know that students who have great intelligence and apply themselves to learning become outstanding people. What Jesus did was learn what could be done and how to do it. He was alert and had good will. When Jesus saw an opportunity to help a needy person, he helped without hesitation.

Jesus became known for his great knowledge, understanding, and wisdom. Because of his ability and good will, the common people loved him and looked up to him.

All the people who were humble and loved truth and had good will wanted to follow Jesus.

The rulers who feared losing their positions were challenged by Jesus. Many who came to know the greatness of Jesus' knowledge, understanding, and wisdom, became jealous of Jesus. Those of ill will came to hate him.

Jesus not only had acquired great knowledge, understanding, and wisdom, but in a relatively short time became famous.

Jesus learned early in life that people were dependent on one another. He came to appreciate the value of peace and harmony, which are necessary for good relations and enjoyable fellowship.

Jesus looked for the best in people and encouraged people to seek the best.

People who knew Jesus came to recognize his superior knowledge and good will.

Jesus became the good people's hero and the bad people's curse. Because of his consistent manner of life, his friends wanted to make Jesus a king and his enemies wanted to destroy him.

The people of good will who knew Jesus considered him to be a Saviour. Those of ill will were determined to destroy him.

Jesus, being one who believes in facing reality and having the wisdom to oppose falsehood, pursued a steady course. He knew that truth or reality triumphs in the end.

Anyone who knows Jesus by having learned his story and applied his teaching knows that his judgement is sound and that by following him we can live a more abundant life.

By accepting Jesus and his teaching we have an ideal to work toward. Following Jesus will save anyone from a life of futility. Those who know Jesus best are his best witnesses.

"Believe in Jesus and make him the Lord of your life," is the only road to perfect peace and future hope. This character and belief in reality are what everyone needs. We need a determination to do what is right and to oppose falsehood as long as we live.

If we will follow Jesus, we will assure the future for those who live after us. When we come to die, we will have no regrets. If we keep our minds on Jesus we will have perfect peace. When we learn to follow Jesus we will overcome death. Death is the mortal enemy. If we accept Jesus and face reality we will live today and trust reality for tomorrow.

If we have good will, a clear conscience, and a perfect example to follow, we have no need for falsehood.

"Know the truth" as taught by Jesus and you will be free from superstition, falsehood, and ill will. And by loving your enemies, you will have no one to hate.

When we teach all people everywhere to follow Jesus, our lives will be whole.

When we follow Jesus we are sane and sober. We will follow and seek reality. When we have no doubts about the future we have prefect peace. (I hope to be in harmony with reality and free from falsehood as long as I live.) Since Jesus is all that I would like to be, he meets all my needs. His grace is sufficient. What is available for me is available for everyone.

The Worship of God

God is a term we use to refer to reality.

Reality or God is what exists or prevails at any given time or place. Reality is the truth that any good, true or just person seeks after. Reality has all power and always endures.

All things work together for good when we face reality with love or good will.

Reality is truth without any falsehood. Reality is what is. God is. God is the revelation that came to Moses. God had Moses say, "The I am has sent you."

To worship God is to attribute worth to truth or reality and to deny any falsehood.

Satan is the term we use to express ultimate falsehood.

God is ultimate truth or reality.

The word or message of God is truth.

The true messenger of God is a messenger that delivers truth.

Reality or truth is always truth. Truth exists now. God's eternity is now.

Reality has no regard for time. "A year is as thousand years or as a day."

Reality never ends and never begins again. It always is.

Reality never changes from being reality.

Reality is what happens regardless of what one thinks of what happens.

Prayer is the sincere desire to find reality and good will.

There is a reality that can solve all problems and heal all diseases.

It is the nature of sane and sober people to seek reality.

Human beings so far as we know are the only animals that communicate and record reality.

Fictitious writings are attempts to picture reality in symbols.

People who are insane are deceived. What seems real is a perception of the mind that is not functioning properly.

No falsehood is reality in the sense of truth. Falsehood is separate from truth. It can never be the whole truth.

Sin is that which is against reality or God.

Sin is less than perfect and always needs to be overcome.

Reality is impartial. God is no respecter of persons.

The Israelites came closer to facing reality than other peoples of their known world.

Idol worship shows a lack of reality on the part of the worshippers.

Reality is not made or created. It is revealed or discovered or it eludes people. Reality rules all time and space. There is no place where reality is not.

The Lord Jesus seeks to reveal God or reality. A true revelation of reality is always redemptive.

With knowledge, understanding, and wisdom, by human beings, who are sane and sober, reality is revealed. Knowledge, understanding, and wisdom can be shared by those who have attained it when they are sane, sober, and of good will.

People who are sane, sober, and informed know the consequence of being false. They know that it is best to face reality.

Reality is identified with law. Everything is subject to law. The law or laws of reality do not change.

When one is against reality, he or she repents or suffers the consequence. One is not punished by reality for sin but by sin. We reap what we sow or what our friends or enemies sow. We cannot mock reality.

By accepting reality we can make progress. It is beyond our imaginations what reality is ahead of us. The righteous face reality. The unrighteous try to hide reality. They choose ignorance because their deeds are evil.

The people of good will seek truth. They face reality. They seek God's will.

When we know truth, we love others and we share truth.

The Church of Christ cannot exclude truth. If a church excludes reality it becomes Satanic.

God Is Reality

God and reality or truth are one concept. God is what is. The verb is, is a verb of being. God is the I am, I was, or I will be.

God is ultimate truth. God is the whole truth and nothing but the truth. Thus we say God cannot lie or be wrong or not be.

God or reality has no beginning and no end. That is why we say that God does not count time. "A day is as a thousand years," or make it a million if you like.

God is an eternal or ever present Spirit. God is seen in nature and animals as life. God is seen in human beings as mental life or thinking capacity.

In the spiritual sense, God as a saving power is the principle of wholeness. The Holy Spirit is wholeness. To desire wholeness, soundness, righteousness and completeness is to be led by the Holy Spirit. It is the same as seeking ultimate truth.

Jesus Christ is the example of truth. To follow Jesus is the same as seeking God or obeying the Spirit or Laws of God. The Trinity - Father, Son, and Holy Spirit are not spiritually different in goals and aspirations. They are expressed as different concepts or different aspects of the truth.

God the Father gives rise to or begets what is.

God the Son reveres or makes known what is.

God the Spirit is the acceptance of the conviction of what is. To be Godly one must completely accept reality and completely reject falsehood.

God is the reality.

Satan is the falsehood.

Jesus reveals the reality by being the perfect example. Jesus is the right way, the whole truth and the life.

Anyway you wish to think, you cannot change what is to what is not. God is reality. Satan is falsehood. The goal of the followers of Jesus is to magnify the real and to do away with the false.

Jesus as the Son of God is the prince of peace. If we follow Jesus we become peacemakers. The peacemakers are called children of God.

Satan as personification of falsehood causes all kinds of havoc.

"All things work together for good to those that love truth and purpose with deepest conviction to pursue it."

Paul, the Apostle of Jesus, tells us to "prove all things and hold on to what is good." Faith is believing what you know to be true and being willing to give your life in the teaching by example of what you are convinced is true.

Jesus allowed himself to be crucified because he had integrity. Jesus is our example. He is Lord and Saviour to those who follow him.

Like Jesus, face reality. Have faith in God. Truth is the only permanent Authority.

Love of Others

The person who believes in one God also believes in one humanity. Such a person is also Christ-like or redemptive. To be Christ-like is to value human life. If we value human life, we desire to be helpful and not harmful.

The sane, sober, and intelligent person of good will always seeks to be helpful to others. To have good will is to love in the Agape sense of the word. All Christ-like or redemptive people have good will.

To have ill will is to be evil or selfish. The person who has ill will or is selfish puts his or her welfare above that of others.

The person of ill will thinks more highly of himself or herself than they ought to think and less highly of others.

The person who is Christ-like or has good will gives the other person what he or she would like the other person to give were the positions exchanged.

If we were all intelligent people of good will we would not have wars, and other causes of suffering would only be for brief periods of time.

The idea of God is the idea of good will. To believe in God is to have good will. God is the reality. Reality is impartial. No human being is exempt from the laws of God or the existing reality. Any concept of special privilege is cultural not natural. The only leveling ingredient is love or good will. This ingredient is made known to us by the learning and thinking process. We promote the learning and thinking through process with objective schools of knowledge.

Through objective or open-minded education we move from

primitivism or savagery to civilization. We move from ignorance and frustration to decency and order. Ignorance and frustration result in chaos. Good discipline or education results in decency and order.

Where we have good will we have self-discipline. Where we have ill will or selfishness we have to have laws and regulations forced on those of ill will so as to have decency and order.

Jesus of Nazareth personifies good will. He shows us through his life and works, including his being a good example and a good teacher, how to bring about decency and order so as to enrich life for all people everywhere.

If we believe in Jesus we can overcome all kinds of chaos. It is yet to be seen how wonderful life can be when we all practice good will or as we say love one another.

Jesus purposed to be a Messiah who would save us from missing the mark in life. He makes it possible for us to live redemptively so that it will have been good for us to have been here. Let's make Jesus Lord.

Covenants

The covenants of God are the agreements between parties that are to be faithfully carried out. A covenant is sealed with one's life. An honest mutual agreement is kept by both parties to the agreement.

The first principle of a covenant is that it must be understood by all concerned. The second principle is that it must be sealed or understood and signed without coercion. The third principle is that it must be delivered or carried out.

When an honest, sensible, sane, and sober person signs a contract he or she is making a good faith agreement. The parties to the agreement stake their reputation on the willingness to keep the covenant.

God is the author of the covenants, which we make with him. God has given us the realities, which we face. The laws of God exist and must be obeyed. These laws control the universe. They are eternal, unchangeable principles. Reality does not change. When we mature or learn enough to know that we cannot change reality or the laws of God; if we are wise, we commit ourselves to obey these laws or as we say to face reality.

It is in obeying the laws or keeping the covenant with God that we are saved from futility or destruction. We have no choice but to obey or perish.

If we try to work against reality we are never at peace or successful.

Jesus Christ reveals to us the laws of God. If we accept Jesus as Lord, we are saved from the destruction of sin. If we reject Jesus we perish. That is to say our efforts are futile when we oppose truth or fight against reality. Jesus is called the Great Teacher because he has learned and taught the laws of God. Jesus associates himself with truth and in opposition to falsehood.

Our idea of God is our concept of reality or truth. God is what is. We who have good will want to know truth or the laws of God. We want to make our lives useful. We are useful to the extent that we help one another. If we obey the truth we become mutually helpful. If we seek or follow falsehood, we become mutually harmful. We cannot be faithful to truth or reality without being helpful.

When one seeks to know and do what is mutually helpful he is a Godly person. When one seeks to be false, he is a Satanic person. God is our conception of what is true and helpful. Satan is our conception of what is false and harmful.

Love that we call Agape or good will is the motive that we have when we are mutually helpful. The true person or follower of Jesus Christ is committed to being helpful to all concerned. The ignorant, the superstitious, the false or those of ill will are harmful to all concerned.

The reality is that there is one God and one people. If we love God, we love truth. If we love truth, we love people. If we love people, we want to help people. Jesus teaches us to love God and to love people.

People who work for mutual benefit are peacemakers. They are called Children of God. They prosper. People who really prosper live rich lives. They love one another. They care for one another. Their joy is in making others happy. They are not greedy or selfish. They live in covenant relationships.

Prayer, In Jesus' Name

I have an entirely different view of prayer from that of many of our leaders.

I accept that teaching of Jesus as I have come to know him

personally. I have been introduced to Jesus by many different people. I rarely find a Bible quoter who knows him.

Bible quoters know what others, the Bible writers in particular, have said about Jesus, but they have never picked the mind of Jesus.

Jesus is not some closed-minded legalist or literalist. Nor is he some prejudiced Southerner from the Bible Belt.

Jesus is not some magician, false god, or political zealot.

Jesus is not some patriot who would kill to protect some national boundary line.

Jesus is not some war god that would give the lives of young men to maintain power.

Jesus is a man who learned early in life to face reality, which we call God.

Jesus reveals this reality or ultimate truth, which we come to know as the laws of God or the unchangeable laws, which govern the universe.

If we believe in and follow Jesus, we learn to relate to one another, to love and help one another so we all live more abundant lives.

Jesus reveals to us the truth about life. Life is always lived between the cradle and the grave. Real life is mental or conscious. It is lived in the now of our time.

The righteous live by faith in reality. The unrighteous choose falsehood.

We say one who denies reality is insane. Jesus taught this truth.

If we follow Jesus, we face reality and do the best we can with what we have where we are in the here and now.

Jesus had an inquiring mind. He desired truth. He looked for answers until he found them.

Jesus was never satisfied with part truth and part falsehood. Jesus wanted the whole truth related to the project or problem at hand.

Jesus was a true scientist. He looked for the reality or God. He looked for the controlling force or truth.

If we follow Jesus we become lifetime learners. We continually look for ways and means to enrich life.

It is evil rather than Christ-like to refuse to learn.

If Jesus were living his earthly life during this age, he would be more like Bill Gates than like many of our preachers. He would do whatever advanced civilization. Primitive people make and use weapons of war. Advanced people make and use means of better communication.

Prayer has to do with planning, communication, and doing things that enrich life for all concerned.

Prayer is an attitude of helpfulness and gratitude.

Prayer is planning, selecting, testing, adjusting, communicating, and serving so as to enrich life.

Prayer is seeking knowledge, understanding, wisdom, and perseverance to mutually help one another.

Prayer is seeking ultimate truth to promote good, better and best relationships.

Prayer is learning how to adjust to situations that arise unexpectedly as well as routine matters.

Prayer is sincere desire to be independent and helpful.

Prayer is seeking to profit from the past, to adjust to the present, and to plan for the future.

Prayer is seeking a full and enjoyable life for all concerned.

Prayer is never seeking an unfair advantage.

Prayer is never seeking to harm anyone.

Prayer is never seeking worldly pleasure.

Prayer is never seeking something for nothing.

Prayer is never hoarding.

Prayer is never breaking the commands of God.

Prayer is never seeking miracles for personal benefit.

Prayer is seeking to recall what we have learned. Prayer is seeking to learn, and seeking to use what we have learned.

Prayer is never seeking credit for what another has done, or for what we haven't done.

Prayer is seeking to live in harmony with the laws of reality or in harmony with God.

Prayer is seeking to be at home with Jesus, even if we have to go there by way of the cross.

Prayer is seeking help as we go from where we are to where we should be. It is what helps us move by stages from faith to more faith as we live as Father Abraham lived. We move forward as long as we are in our right minds.

God is Truth

God is truth. God is reality. God is the embodiment of all the unchangeable laws, which govern the universe. God is not subject to created things, but he is the principal by which all things come into being. God is the ultimate truth that all learners seek after. God is the truth that frees us from all ignorance, superstition, and all other falsehoods.

No man made culture is equal to God. The most any culture can achieve is an idea of perfection. Human beings do not live long enough to learn everything. Before a truth can be known as truth and absorbed into a culture it must be tried and proved to be effective. God is known by faith. The person or persons who are faithful are those who do what they have found to be helpful in enriching life. They are not only teachers and talkers; they are doers.

Faithful ministers are examples of what they preach or teach. They share the truth.

Faithful ministers never try to exploit other human beings. They do not think of themselves as being special. They recognize that they may be given special duties, but they are never exempt from any of the laws of truth. God's laws or the truth applies to all. "It rains on the just and the unjust." "Truth is no respecter of persons."

The good citizen seeks to obey the customs of his culture in order to live in harmony with others. However, the good citizen seeks truth. If the culture is against truth, the one who knows truth seeks to change his or her culture to conform to truth. The sensible and sane and sober individual makes sure he or she is being helpful and not just being rebellious. The goal should be to obey truth and to overcome falsehood so as to be in obedience to unchangeable, underlying principles.

Jesus is our example. He tried to change what was wrong or false to what was right or true. To Jesus repentance was always turning from the false to the true. Satan personifies the false. God personifies truth.

The righteous never need to repent. The righteous always give truth the authority. Authority is always truth. For an individual or group to seek power, honor, or prestige so as to manipulate or rule is always based on falsehood. True greatness and true authority comes from truth. Humility or willingness to learn is the path of truth.

The "Great Commission" is a command to make learners and to obey the laws of God. We are to make learners of truth who will obey the laws of God so as to bring about abundant life.

The Kingdom of God is a Kingdom of truth. The Kingdom of Satan is the reign of falsehood.

When we believe in Jesus enough to learn and obey the truth, we will be saved from the reign of falsehood. Jesus gave his life that we may know truth and be set free from falsehood.

If we accept Jesus as Lord we begin to see that truth is self-evident. Reality or God is consistent. God as the manifestation of truth can be trusted. Not to trust reality is foolish, if not insanity or ignorance. To trust in falsehood is to miss the mark or be guilty of sin. "The wages of sin is death." The gift of God–knowledge of truth, is the pathway to life. The last enemy to be destroyed is death. Death is the fruit of falsehood. Life is the fruit of truth.

A Miracle

If one interprets a notable happening that is a bit unusual to be a miracle, then there are many miracles. If one interprets a miracle to be contrary to the laws of God, then there are no miracles. There are laws that control the universe, which are dependable. These laws are called laws because they do not change.

Jesus always faced truth. He interpreted anything and everything contrary to truth to be falsehood and therefore evil. Anyone seeking something contrary to the laws of God is doing evil.

The righteous people seek to know truth. The only way to be righteous is to live by the truth of God. To believe what is true and to live by what is true is to be faithful. To doubt what is true and to seek some falsehood is to be unfaithful.

If we live by faith we have to be willing to suffer at times. To live by faith means to face reality or as we say to trust God. The righteous face truth and obey the laws of God. The wicked seek some falsehood when the going gets tough. God is reality. Satan is falsehood. To seek some falsehood so as to escape reality is evil or Satanic.

Instead of seeking truth and obeying God's laws the wicked disobey God's laws by refusing to learn and obey them. When we neglect our health and our bodies become weak and degenerate, we suffer the consequences of our sins. At such times we seek some so-called miracle cure. We would like to change reality, but reality cannot change. Seeking to change God's laws is seeking falsehood.

The righteous person confesses his sins and tries to make amends. The wicked person tries to escape punishment. Instead of paying his debts the evil person seeks a miracle. He would like for the law of sin and retribution to change. The only remedy for sin is repentance. To repent is to turn from falsehood to truth.

Righteous people seek truth. We want to live in obedience to God's eternal unchangeable laws. We do not mock God by trying to create new laws. We know that we reap what we sow.

Jesus did not die so we could live in falsehood. Jesus died so that we would be willing to suffer for truth. Jesus makes no attempt to escape reality. Jesus makes it possible for us to face reality. If we believe in Jesus we do not seek falsehood as an escape hatch. We confess our sins, repent of all falsehood and seek truth. We pay our honest debts. The only debt we should owe is our debt of love for one another. We should always love others. We never pay our debt of love. To live truth is to keep on loving or showing good will. Faith in God and good will are closely related. Faith and good will are based on truth.

To turn from falsehood to truth is to turn from Satan unto God. "Be not deceived, God or truth is not mocked, whatsoever we sow, we shall reap." "Obedience is better than sacrifice." If you believe in God, you will face reality. If you are evil, you will seek to replace reality with falsehood. We are to trust God. "I will repay says the Lord."

When we pay our debts, God forgives and it is as though we had never owed. Repentance comes before forgiveness. To follow Jesus is to be honest and true.

Live by Faith

The righteous live by faith. To live by faith means to learn what needs to be done and to persevere in doing it. Faith is the exercise of the mind and body to plan and carry out what we believe will enhance the lives of all concerned.

A small task requires little faith. An important task requires much faith. Whatever the task, the faihful who have wisdom seek to obey the laws of God, which are the truth or reality.

Great people plan their work and work their plans. Wise people have integrity and good will. They visualize the task and see in their mind the finished building or project before they begin the permanent work. A worthwhile project has to be carefully planned.

As with King Solomon building a temple or a palace, one must have authority and resources to do a great task. All concerned must be in harmony if the task is to be done right. Material for the task must be acquired, methods of transportation, workmen to be involved, and ways and means of finishing the project. Those involved in doing a task must have the skills for the task. There must also be proper supervision. The leader or leaders have to decide who will do what, when, where and how. Plans must be made and costs counted. The project must serve the purpose for which it is intended.

A life to be successful is like a project or a task. A life should be lived with purpose. It should be integrated and helpful to all concerned. One lives in relationships. No one lives alone or dies alone in the overall sense. We are all part of one humanity.

Wise people of maturity, good sense, and good will seek to live in harmony with others. A sane, sensible, and sober adult will seek what is best for all concerned. This means a lot of learning and self-discipline. Good people are responsible people. We accept responsibility for our behavior.

The responsible person does what needs to be done when it needs to be done. The responsible person is led by mind or Spirit. He or she does not let emotions, pleasures, and lusts of the flesh or pride or greed dominate their behavior.

The truly happy person lives according to the principles taught by the life and works of Jesus of Nazareth which are written about in Christian literature and elsewhere.

To live a happy, useful, and satisfying life requires effort as well as authority and ability. The only real authority is truth or reality, which I call God. The opposite or enemy of God is falsehood, which is a synonym for Satan or devil. All truth is to be sought after, praised, and cherished. All falsehood is to be shunned. Truth lengthens and strengthens life. Falsehood destroys.

We will bring about a better world when we accept Jesus Christ as Lord. To accept Jesus Christ as Lord is to let truth or God dominate one's life. To reject Jesus is to choose falsehood as lord. To choose truth is to choose to be saved from ignorance, superstition, and all other false notions.

It has been rightly said, "To yourself be true and you cannot be false to anyone." If one is honest with himself or herself, he or she has integrity. A person of integrity is reliable; he or she pays his or her debts; he or she lives by faith; and he or she has good will or loves others.

Believe in the Lord Jesus Christ and you will be saved from falsehood; you will experience truth and be free of guilt.

Prayer (2)

The one to be prayed for makes a request for prayer. He or she requests the prayer to pray for them because he or she believes in the prayer of the one praying. The person is helped if they have faith and respond to the prayer.

We cannot pray random prayers. Prayer without faith isn't real. We may gather together and pray for one another, but we cannot pray for the whole world. To pray for people who do not have faith is just seeking vain glory.

A sincere prayer is, Lord I believe, help my unbelief, give me more faith. When people act like the Pharisees and pray long prayers to be seen of others they are foolish.

A sincere prayer is a sincere request by one who has faith.

Jesus taught his disciples to pray when they requested him to do so. Jesus prayed for people's requests to be granted. The requests were granted to those who had faith. It wasn't the prayer that healed, it was the faith of the one requesting the prayer.

If saying prayers would heal people we could heal everybody. It takes faith and obedience to be healed.

We should maintain an attitude of prayer and pray for those who request prayer.

The prayer must believe in reality. He or she must pray for truth or reality. It does no good to seek the impossible. You cannot be serious and have faith if you do not believe you can make things happen. You cannot ask God to break or violate his laws.

If you believe you can move a mound of dirt into the sea, you can do it. But don't ask for the stars to fall.

Prayers are answered for people who agree in regards to what they want done. If you have doubts, you can't pray. Unless you can make decisions you cannot pray or be sincere. Prayer is having sincere desire. When we have sincere desire, we exercise faith.

It is God's will that his people work in unity and that they seek knowledge, understanding, and wisdom. The unstable, wishy-washy cannot expect anything from the Lord. If we refuse to seek knowledge, understanding, and wisdom, we are not serious enough to have faith. The fool acts as if there is no reality.

If we want to change things, we need to come to agreement or consensus. Prayer is not mere words that sound good. Prayer is sincere desire to do good.

The best way to stimulate prayer is to seek to meet human need. No one prays who doesn't love people enough to help meet their needs.

No one can pray for himself or herself unless they have a need that they are seriously trying to meet.

People who believe in Jesus pray without ceasing. They sincerely seek to meet needs and solve problems. The more urgent the need, the more sincere the prayer.

When people pray long prayers, they are not sincere. Such people are hypocrites. They act as if words could replace deeds. They act as if falsehood could replace truth. Prayer does not change the reality or truth. Prayer helps sincere people to face truth. Truth has a healing effect. Whereas falsehood causes more havoc.

If we confess our sins, we tend to overcome them. If we pretend to be righteous when we are not, our sins increase. Wise people learn to mean what they say. Fools use many empty words. The most offensive fools are those who talk much and convey little meaning.

When others request us to pray for them, they are in need of prayer and they believe in prayer, and they show faith in us. They are also willing to work with us.

Be sincere, a prayer is a work garment. Ask for what you are ready to work toward.